Table of Contents

P9-APP-115

Introduction
    Wornie L. Reed 1

Critique of Chapter 5, "Black Political Participation"
    Susan Welch 7

Critique of Chapter 6, "Blacks in the Economy"
    Herbert Hill 13

Critique of Chapter 7, "The Schooling of Black Americans"
    Antoine M. Garibaldi 23

Critique of Chapter 8, "Black Americans' Health"
    William A. Darity, Sr. 27

Critique of Chapter 9, "Crime and the Administration of
Criminal Justice"
    E. Yvonne Moss 35

Critique of Chapters 6 and 10, "Blacks in the Economy" and
"Children and Families"
    Robert B. Hill and James B. Stewart 41

The Status of African-Americans: Convergence or
Divergence?
    James B. Stewart 45

Appendix: Assessment of the Status of African-Americans
Project Study Group Members 55

Critiques of the NRC Study,
A Common Destiny:
Blacks and American Society
Volume VI

Edited by Wornie L. Reed

William Monroe Trotter Institute

University of Massachusetts at Boston

1990

Introduction

Wornie L. Reed

In 1984 the National Research Council (NRC) of the National Academy of Sciences began a study on the status of black Americans. Black Americans are plagued by problems. These problems include unemployment, under-employment, poverty, crime, and poor health. The gap between blacks and whites in economic status is not closing. Consequently, there is a great need to examine trends, evaluate programs, and recommend social policies to address these problems. So, five years ago, with $2 million in funding from foundations, the NRC began a study to report on the status of blacks from 1940 to the present and on the *future status of blacks in the United States.*

The NRC study, which was billed as an update of Gunnar Myrdal's study, *An American Dilemma,* has since its inception faced severe criticisms. Many critics complained about the limited involvement of black scholars in the conceptualization, planning, and development of the project. They noted that many black scholars who are prominent in some of the areas under study were conspicuously omitted from the study panels.

Since the NRC study was intended as an update of the Myrdal study, it might be useful to review the Myrdal work. Gunnar Myrdal was recruited to direct that study from Sweden, a country with no history of colonization and no apparent vested interest in the history of black-white relations. The work, which was published in 1944, reigned for nearly a quarter of a century as the authoritative study of black life in the United States. There was no competing major study.

In a masterfully crafted argument Myrdal concluded that the racial oppression of blacks in America was the result of an American conflict, an American dilemma: the discrepancy between an egalitarian ideology and racially discriminatory behavior. However, while he addressed the real issue–racial oppression–he presented it in combination with a very positive statement about America–about the American Creed, thereby making his overall assessment of racial problems more palatable to his audience.

An American Dilemma became a classic within American social science, and it reached a broad readership. For two decades it was the definitive survey of black Americans. Civil rights activists, ministers, teachers, and social workers used the book as a reference in their struggles against segregation.

In spite of its widespread influence in the black community, as well as in the Northern white community, the study had its black critics. Many questioned whether racism could be reduced by addressing the contradiction in America's conscience. Some social scientists argued that Myrdal paid too little attention to institutional racism, and that the elimination of racial discrimination and domination would require institutional change and addressing social structural problems. On the other hand, liberal social scientists were reluctant to criticize a book that forcefully condemned racism and spread this message to a wide audience.

In a significant critique, novelist Ralph Ellison applauded the book but situated the Myrdal study in a historical line of social science writings that had done more to maintain the status quo for blacks than to change it. Oliver Cox was another prominent critic. He argued that in studying social problems it was important to examine the relationship between social problems and social structure.

Concerned about some of the issues raised about the manner in which the NRC study team was established, the William Monroe Trotter Institute initiated a parallel study with the intention of widening the discussion of the current situation of African-Americans and the social policy implications of that condition. In the spring of 1987 the Trotter Institute initiated the project, "The Assessment of the Status of African-Americans." Thirty-five scholars were organized into study groups, one for each of six topics: education; employment, income, and occupations; political participation and the administration of justice; social and cultural change; health status and medical care; and the family. The study groups were established to analyze in a parallel study–but obviously on a smaller scale than the NRC study–the status of African-Americans in each of the topical areas in anticipation of the results and analyses of the NRC's Study Committee on the Status of Black Americans.

The multidisciplinary group of scholars comprising the study groups of the Trotter Institute study included persons from all sections of the country and from varied settings–private and public universities, historically black colleges and universities, and private agencies; and it included white as well as black scholars. The 35 study group members–with the assistance of 26 other scholars who made a variety of contributions, including original papers, reprints, notes and materials, and/or substantial commentaries on draft documents–developed a six-volume study.[1] This, the sixth volume, is a set of critiques of the NRC study, *A Common Destiny: Blacks and the American Society*, by some of the members of the Trotter Institute study groups.

The NRC Study

The NRC study provides much useful data and some important conclusions. One conclusion concerns discrimination:

Foremost among the reasons for the present state of black-white relations are two continuing consequences of the nation's long and recent history of racial inequality. One is the negative attitudes held toward blacks and the other is the actual disadvantaged conditions under which many black Americans live. These two consequences reinforce each other. Thus, a legacy of discrimination and segregation continues to affect black-white relations. (p. 5)

Another noteworthy conclusion from the NRC study is its refutation of blaming-the-victim arguments for the persistence of poverty among black Americans:

> [T]he evidence does not support some popular hypotheses that purport to explain female-headed households, high birth rates to unmarried women, low labor force participation by males, or poor academic performance solely on the basis of government support programs or, more generally, on the existence of a "culture of poverty" among the black poor. (p. 10)

The NRC study also found that the sharp rise in single-parent families was *not* a significant factor in the increase in poverty among blacks in the 1970s.

Although there are reasons to commend the NRC study, there are also a number of problems with the study. The study looked at the situation of blacks in America, it raised issues of discrimination, but it never examined the extent to which institutions of society help or hinder the progress of blacks. In fact, the study appears to deny the existence of such institutional effects:

> [A] considerable amount of remaining black-white inequality is due to continuing discriminatory treatment of blacks. *However, direct evidence of systematic discriminatory behavior by whites is difficult to obtain.* [Emphasis added]
> (p. 155)

This is an incredible statement, and it accurately reflects the orientation of the study. Racial discrimination is seen to exist, but only in the dimension of individual action. No consideration is given to the widely accepted "extra-individual" effect: institutional racism.

Another problematic aspect of *A Common Destiny* is the use of the period around 1940 as the baseline point of reference. In 1940 most African-Americans-especially those living in the South–were living in a state of virtual apartheid. They could not participate in many of the institutions of society: most could not vote or use the public library, many could not even walk in a city park–and the list goes on. African-Americans living in the North were also severely restricted. A more useful point of reference–as suggested by data presented in the study–is the mid-1960s, after the passage of the Civil Rights Act of 1964 and the Voting Rights Act of 1965.

The Nature of Black Participation in American Society

The NRC study examined the participation of blacks in a wide range of American institutions. They show that in those areas where the government has played an activist and interventionist role, as in the military, there is a high degree of desegregation. They argue that the military is perhaps the most successful institution for integration, with the army leading the way. But by their own definition, though desegregation has been increased in the military, integration has not been attained–integration being defined as fair representation in terms of numbers, equal status with whites, and *participation in making decisions.* Only in the army, with 10% black officers, is there anything approaching racial representation in the officer ranks. And, of course, few of these black officers are at the very high ranks.

The part of the study that discussed identity and institutions in the black community had some key omissions. It recounted the development of the civil rights movement, the NAACP, and the National Urban League, and it dealt–although a good deal less thoroughly–with the Southern Christian Leadership Conference (SCLC) and the Student Non-Violent Coordination Committee (SNCC). However, it generally avoided post-1960s political development. For instance, there is no treatment of the various forms of community and political organizations that emerged in the 1960s, no mention of the Black Panther Party, and no mention of community movements for control of schools and control of police. Although the Nation of Islam is discussed as a move towards self-determination, none of the other movements in that direction is discussed. How these new movements in the post-1960-65 period transformed the political landscape of the black community and our social consciousness received little attention.

The NRC study speaks of black-white residential segregation as perhaps the most vexing problem in American race relations. Considering the data, one can see why. Using a segregation index (where 100 would mean complete segregation and zero would mean complete integration), for the 29 metropolitan areas with the largest black populations, the index was 77 in 1980, not much changed from 81 in 1970 and 80 in 1960. If black-white residential segregation continued to decline at the rate it declined in the 1970s it would take over 150 years to achieve complete integration. In fact, it would take five or six decades for blacks to reach the levels of residential segregation now observed among Hispanics and Asian-Americans, which is about 50. The NRC study could have served a more useful function by examining the causes of phenomena such as this.

References

1.   Reed, W.L. (Ed.). (1989). *Summary.* Vol. 1 of *Assessment of the Status of African-Americans.* Boston: William Monroe Trotter Institute, University of Massachusetts.

Hill, R.B., et al. (Eds.). (1989). *Research on the African-American Family.* Vol. 2 of *Assessment of the Status of African-Americans.* Boston: William Monroe Trotter Institute, University of Massachusetts.

Willie, C.V., Garibaldi, A.M., & Reed, W.L. (Eds.). (1990). *The Education of African-Americans.* Vol. 3 of *Assessment of the Status of African-Americans.* Boston: William Monroe Trotter Institute, University of Massachusetts.

Reed, W.L. (Ed.). (1990). *Social, Political, and Economic Issues in Black America.* Vol. 4 of *Assessment of the Status of African-Americans.* Boston: William Monroe Trotter Institute, University of Massachusetts.

Reed, W.L. (Ed.). (1990). *Health and Medical Care of African-Americans.* Vol. 5 of *Assessment of the Status of African-Americans.* Boston: William Monroe Trotter Institute, University of Massachusetts.

Reed, W.L. (Ed.). (1990). *Critiques of National Research Council's Study, A Common Destiny.* Vol. 6 of *Assessment of the Status of African-Americans.* Boston: William Monroe Trotter Institute, University of Massachusetts.

Wornie L. Reed is director of the William Monroe Trotter Institute and chair of the Black Studies Department at the University of Massachusetts at Boston. He directed the Trotter Institute's study on the status of African-Americans.

Critique of Chapter 5,
"Black Political Participation"

Susan Welch
with the Study Group on Political Participation

There is much to commend in chapter 5's extensive review of the research on many forms of black political participation. The chapter draws together findings on diverse aspects of participation–from protest to office holding–and these findings are treated in a coherent way. It even-handedly examines and summarizes a wide variety of literature. It will be a useful resource for students and scholars alike.

Despite these virtues, the chapter lacks the kind of insight and synthesis that will help us answer the question, "Where do we go from here?" It makes no attempt to reach a conclusion about the meaning of the descriptive findings. What does the research ultimately say about blacks' role in American politics and how blacks might use that role to obtain a more equal place in society? There is no sense of a theme or conclusion that might be of use in either understanding blacks' status in society or seeking to change that status. If these goals were important ones in commissioning the NRC study, the chapter is a classic example of missing the forest for the trees.

To bear out this assertion, we will first discuss some of the analytic and interpretive problems found in the chapter. We will then turn to a consideration of how the chapter's findings might have been used to reach some broader conclusions about the steps that need to be taken to bring blacks to a more equal status in society.

Analytic and Interpretive Problems

Analytic Problems

While the magnitude of this study should have led to a careful reporting of the most up-to-date surveys and other data, such current information is generally missing from this chapter. For example, opinions drawn from the General Social Surveys, conducted by the National Opinion Research Commission, are not updated beyond what the researchers found in previously published articles (see for example, tables 5-3, 5-4, 5-5). Nor are current figures on black representation provided, such as black delegates to the 1988 National Political Convention (table 5-6) or black elected officials since 1985 (tables 5-10, 5-11). All of this data is readily available at research universities across the nation. Thus, much important trend data from the second term of the Reagan administration is omitted. Similarly, in the discussion of policy issues, consideration of the Reagan era and its impact on government policy is curiously minimal.

Core Political Values

The chapter appropriately discusses core political values, and it does a thorough job in comparing black and white attitudes toward capitalism and inequality, and towards governmental efforts to redistribute resources. But the discussion is limited in that it largely ignores the core political values of the larger society. Black political activity operates within the context of the larger polity; restricting the discussion primarily to core political values of blacks fails to take account of how those values and views square with the values shaping the opinions and actions of Americans generally, that is white Americans. A treatment of core political values should discuss values and beliefs such as individualism, equality, majority rule and minority rights, and should discuss how these concepts affect the role of minority groups such as blacks.[1]

Also ignored is the American attachment to legalism and legal forms, as well as to compromise as the appropriate remedy for conflict. These beliefs greatly influence the current status of blacks, and they also influence the nature of possible remedies for inequality. It was by contrasting the status of blacks with stated American values that Gunnar Mrydal's study, *An American Dilemma*, became a classic. The NRC study, by contrast, lacks a perspective on how core American values and beliefs have influenced the nation's development, and in so doing have influenced the political and social status of blacks.

The core political values section also suffers from a failure to consider the larger institutional context in which black politics operates. We need to understand "the rules of the game" and their influence upon who plays the game and who wins it. Political scientists have demonstrated that the rules and structures of politics are not neutral; certain interests are advantaged and certain others disadvantaged by structural change—as the NRC authors acknowledge when they discuss election rules in local government. As Barker and McCorry have argued, "Federalism, separation of powers, and checks and balances reflect the diversity of interests in American politics . . . they also institutionalize and preserve the prevailing rather than aspiring interests. They promote incremental and marginal change rather than decisive and fundamental change."[2] These institutional features are crucial in understanding why political change comes slowly, if at all.

The discussion of blacks and the political parties (pp. 216-218) does not deal fully enough with the problems blacks encounter in the two-party system. A more direct discussion of the nature, influence, and impact of the two-party system on black political participation is needed. Like other features of American politics, the two-party system engenders moderation, compromise, and incremental change, characteristics that militate against the fundamental, decisive policy changes needed to overcome the serious socioeconomic problems facing black—along with many white—Americans. Because the chapter focuses primarily on black political values, black politics, and the black community generally, it minimizes and in some cases overlooks the impact of system rules and structures that relate powerfully to the current problems of black Americans and to the strategies for addressing those problems.

In terms of black core values the chapter seeks to establish that blacks are not self-declared liberals. Their argument here seems forced since most previous work has shown that blacks do tend to see themselves as liberal, even though more blacks than whites decline to place themselves on this scale. Indeed, the attitudinal patterns displayed in the chapter itself are clearly liberal when considered within the American political context. In terms of opinions about governmental spending, for example, the lowest level of black support (for welfare) is approximately the same as the highest level of white support for spending in any category except crime control.

The Struggle for Civil Rights

The section on the struggle for civil rights provides a useful, if brief, summary of the Civil Rights Movement, incorporating recent scholarship into the account. But the chapter minimizes the central role of protest in bringing about many of the most important social and political advances of blacks,[3] and is silent on the subject of current and future possibilities of redress of black grievances. The chapter also gives less space than warranted to some of the most contemporary civil rights issues. A major current issue in voting rights is minority vote dilution–accomplished through structural arrangements that make it difficult for minorities to elect the representatives of their choice.[4] This issue is treated in the most abbreviated fashion, and relatively little evidence is presented.

Voting and Holding Office

The problem of nonvoting by citizens of all races, which is now very much on the national agenda, is not significantly addressed in this chapter.[5] Again, this may reflect the inattention to the larger political system that we have already noted. Data on the relationship between urban political structures and black representation is now about a decade old, and though the authors of the chapter cannot be expected to be current on studies presented only at professional conventions, they should have noted that the black role in urban politics has increased dramatically over the past decade. Indeed, while it is still clear that blacks are more proportionally represented in district systems than in at-large systems, the representation gap between the two systems found in the 1970s has narrowed considerably in the 1980s.[6]

Influencing Public Policy

A number of policy areas are treated, though superficially. The comments made on local politics are appropriate, especially the question raised as to whether black elected officials should focus on increasing opportunities for black professionals or on redistributive policies. There is, however, much more that needs to be said with regard to black influence on policymaking and on the desirable outcomes of that influence.

Conclusions: Toward a Bigger Picture

Despite its competence as a review of the literature, this chapter was disappointing in its failure to provide a historical framework for blacks' current standing and its failure to explore what strategies might be adopted to bring about a more equal society. Part of the reason for these omissions is the lack of a broader context for the discussion of black participation and values. Black participation and values do not exist independent of more general American values, institutions, and processes. The biases inherent in American political institutions are of prime relevance to the status of blacks.

Another important contextual factor, noticeable in its omission, is American diversity. The United States is becoming increasingly diverse, so diverse that within 20 years blacks might not even be the largest minority group. What are the implications of this for the status of blacks and for strategies to bring about a change in that status? In the face of increasing numbers of nonwhite and non-English speaking minorities, should blacks seek a "rainbow coalition," as advocated by Jesse Jackson, or will blacks find more success in coalitions with the dominant group? While we have no certain answers to these questions, any serious attempts to address the status of blacks in 1989 must at least consider them. Perhaps increased diversity will muffle the black-white conflict that has been the hallmark of American politics for centuries. Or perhaps it will exacerbate it if blacks see first- and second-generation Americans moving ahead of them on the socioeconomic ladder.[7]

Yet another contextual factor to which little attention was paid in the chapter is federalism. Federalism allows multiple points of decision and hence multiple points for political pressure. The distribution of blacks within cities, states, and the nation as a whole leads to the obvious conclusion that blacks have more potential and actual political clout in some areas than others. Some cities have black majorities, others only a handful of blacks. Some states–Maryland, Georgia, North Carolina, South Carolina, Alabama, Mississippi, and Louisiana–have black populations comprising over 20% of the population, while in others–Maine, Vermont, South Dakota, and Montana–blacks are less than .5%. Nationwide, blacks comprise 11% of the population. These differing proportions suggest that strategies for black political success, both in terms of influencing policy and getting blacks elected to office, will differ from one location to another. The kind of political clout that blacks can exercise in Cleveland is more significant than in any state, even those with the highest proportion of blacks. And the kind of clout that blacks can exercise in many states is stronger than at the national level. These are rather simple statements, yet they have significant implications. Strategies that work in one context simply will not work in others because the power base is not there.

The question of desirable coalitions and desirable policy objectives was largely glossed over in the NRC study's chapter on black political participation. Some of the features described in the chapter cry out for recommendations. For example, while it is accurate to point out that black voter turnout is not much lower than white–and in some categories it is higher than whites–is it not more important to comment on the fact that the American electorate is becoming increasingly middle and upper class? Voting rates of working-class whites and working-class blacks are shrinking. Doesn't this situation call for drastic action? Shouldn't we work to bring Americans of all races back into the electorate? Congress is considering mail registration, agency registration, and other proposals to make registration less of a burden on voters. These plans should be endorsed and worked for by those who believe in a representative government, one that incorporates the working and the lower classes of all races.

Many white Americans are concerned about such issues as expanding moderate-cost housing, relieving underemployment, improving local schools, finding a way to send their children to college, and other issues of vital importance to blacks. To bring about improvements in these areas, allies in the white community are essential. Policy proposals in these areas that are seen by the public as benefiting primarily blacks have little chance of passage or successful implementation. Other policy areas suggest other strategies. Those interested in black equality must continue their fight against electoral institutions that deprive blacks of a chance to elect their own representatives. Changing electoral structures will not necessarily require a broad base of white support; in many instances, logical allies are other racial and ethnic minorities.

In sum, the National Research Council provided a useful survey of a large body of literature on black participation, but they failed to put it in a context that illuminates either today's problems or tomorrow's solutions. Nor did they draw conclusions from the descriptive data. As Lucius Barker has commented, "The time has come when much more than data accumulation and description. . .is needed." We need to move beyond description to focus on "what these studies suggest about the way we do things in American politics, and what should be done to. . .achieve racial justice."[8]

References

1.   Drawn primarily from a personal communication to me by L. Barker.

2.   Barker, L. & McCorry, J. (1980). *Black Americans and the Political System.* Boston: Little Brown and Company. P. 76.

3.   Personal communication with L. Barker.

4.   Davison, C., Ed. (1984). *Minority Vote Dilution.* Washington, DC: Howard University Press.

5.   Piven, F.F. & Cloward, R.A. (1988). *Why Americans Don't Vote.* New York: Pantheon.

6.   Welch, S. (1989). The Impact of At-Large Elections on the Representation of Blacks and Hisanics on Urban Councils. Unpublished paper. Welch S. & Herrick, R. (1989). The Impact of Election Structures on the Representation of Black and White Women on Urban Councils. Paper presented at the 1989 meeting of the Midwest Political Science Association, April, Chicago, IL.

7.   To some extent this is already happening. Asian-Americans outdo white as well as black Americans in many areas of educational and occupational achievement. Studies of Hispanic Americans find them subject to fewer discriminatory actions than blacks.

8.   Personal communications with L. Barker.

Susan Welch is the Carl Happold Professor of Political Science at the University of Nebraska, Lincoln.

Critique of Chapter 6, "Blacks in the Economy"

Herbert Hill

"Blacks in the Economy," chapter 6 of the National Research Council (NRC) report *A Common Destiny: Blacks and American Society*, is largely a compilation of information from sources concerned with the quantification of data. The chapter does not provide a new analysis or an original interpretation of the factors responsible for the economic condition of the black population. It consists of a review of some of the published research on the improving status of blacks from 1940 to 1973 and on the declining status of blacks since that time. The chapter concludes that the improvements in economic status were due largely to an expanding economy, demographic developments, and civil rights programs.

Much emphasis is given to the concept that an expanding economy is the decisive factor in achieving black economic progress. While recapitulating the conclusions of various research projects, the report implicitly minimizes the significance of institutionalized racism, i.e., entrenched patterns of occupational segregation and other forms of job discrimination that operate to benefit whites at the expense of blacks. As the extensive record of litigation under Title VII, the employment section of the Civil Rights Act of 1964, demonstrates, such practices are as prevalent in prosperity as in recession. Vigorously defended, these practices remain impervious to change until challenged in protracted and costly court cases brought by black plaintiffs. Throughout the NRC report race and racism are dealt with as conceptual abstraction. With its emphasis on quantification of economic data, the report lacks historical perspective on the relationship between race and economics. The essential context for an effective analysis, the racial oppression of blacks, is missing from this study.

An underlying assumption that permeates much of this chapter is that race is of declining significance, this though the data suggests that a general improvement in the economy will do little for the black underclass or the black working poor. These categories exist not simply because of social injustice and blind economic forces, they exist as a direct consequence of generations of employment discrimination and therefore require race-specific remedies. The NRC report tends to remove job discrimination and the problems of black workers from their historical and institutional context, and thus the report either ignores or minimizes the role of racism in the creation and perpetuation of pervasive economic disparities.

For example, the black working poor who have existed for generations in increasing numbers in black communities across the country receive exactly two paragraphs in chapter 6 (page 283). These paragraphs consist of data taken from two reports by the same researchers. The subject is disposed of with the conclusion that all working poor families "have suffered disproportionately," and "since blacks are disproportionately found in low wage jobs, they are likely to be particularly affected."

A major omission in chapter 6 is the failure to examine in primary sources the role of government agencies in enforcing legal prohibitions against employment discrimination. A subsection entitled "Equal Employment Opportunity Enforcement" does not in fact discuss the serious problem of securing government enforcement of the two most important legal instruments in this area: Title VII, the employment section of the Civil Rights Act of 1964, and the federal Executive Orders prohibiting job discrimination by government contractors. Instead, most of this sub-section (pages 315-319) is devoted to summaries of various attempts to measure the economic effects of these legal prohibitions. But the economic impact will be determined by whether and how effectively the law is enforced. The mere proclamation of civil rights law changes nothing; the issue of enforcement is decisive.

Failure to actively enforce on a sustained basis results in the administrative nullification of antidiscrimination law. But the issue of governmental enforcement is not substantively discussed. Here is the report's concluding sentence: "General changes in race relations, educational improvement, the state of the economy, and government policies that facilitate these factors and provide incentives for the equal employment opportunity of minorities have each had an important role in determining blacks' labor market status" (page 319). Nor has the commentary leading up to this been markedly less general.

According to the report, "The paramount achievement of the civil rights movement in this field was the Civil Rights Act of 1964, which outlawed discrimination in all aspects of employment" (p. 319). While the report implicitly indicates that the potential of employment discrimination law has not been realized, there is no substantive examination of the functioning of the Equal Employment Opportunity Commission and the Office of Federal Contract Compliance Programs, the federal agencies responsible respectively for enforcing Title VII of the Civil Rights Act and the Executive Orders.

An extensive documentation, including investigative reports from other government agencies, describes in detail the failure of the federal government to enforce the principal legal prohibitions against job discrimination. This issue is of great importance and has many implications for a study of the economic status of blacks, especially since the government directly and indirectly subsidizes racial discrimination in violation of the law in major sectors of the economy. But these and related issues are not discussed in chapter 6 of the NRC report.

In October 1988, the United States General Accounting Office released a detailed report to Congress based on its most recent investigation of the functioning and effectiveness of the Equal Employment Opportunity Commission (EEOC).[1] Previous critical reports had been made to Congress in 1976, 1981, 1986, and 1987.[2] Each of these revealed serious inadequacies in the enforcement of Title VII, but the 1988 study, in conjunction with other documentation including the EEOC's own reports, confirms the conclusion that the commission as it has been operating is incapable of enforcing the law.

In reality the EEOC operates as a claims adjustment bureau, not as a law enforcement agency. The commission seeks voluntary, negotiated settlements with emphasis upon the quick resolution of issues, usually by extended compromise and the acceptance of a minimal accommodation to Title VII requirements. As a result there is no genuine conciliation, little threat of litigation, and minimal substantive compliance with the statute. Major national corporation and labor unions have come to understand that paying money in settlement agreements is often a way of disposing of all claims, past, present, and future, while buying a license to continue the discriminatory pattern with minimum of alterations. These and other practices of the EEOC vitiate the enforcement of Title VII.

The commission does not operate with the understanding that patterns of occupational stratification and discrimination are the consequence of group subordination, not the result of individual, random acts of malevolence. The significance of Title VII is in its potential to provide class-wide relief and to eliminate institutionalized patterns of discrimination. But because the agency rejects the idea that Title VII was meant to be an instrument for social change, the EEOC does not enforce the law as amended by Congress in 1972. Historians are certain to regard this record as a classic example of administrative nullification of a civil rights statute.

Seventeen years after Congress amended Title VII and gave the EEOC the power to litigate and to attack systemic patterns of employment discrimination, the commission has been responsible for less than 10% of all Title VII litigation. This figure includes interventions, amicus briefs, and subpoena actions by the EEOC. Virtually all of the significant litigation under Title VII has been initiated and conducted by the private civil rights bar, in a series of major cases that have brought significant relief to large numbers of workers. But the potential of the Civil Rights Act in eliminating discriminatory employment patterns can never be realized if enforcement depends largely on the action of civil rights organizations, whose resources are limited rather than on action by the government itself. Private enforcement of the law by victims of discrimination is totally inadequate. Given this record, there is of course great irony in the fact that U.S. courts of appeals have on more than one occasion stated that "the Equal Employment Opportunity Commission is the primary enforcement mechanism of Title VII." [3]

The authority to initiate lawsuits under the "pattern or practice" provision of Section 707 is potentially the most important power the EEOC acquired under the 1972 Amendments. The many judicial opinions that define the nature of employment discrimination clearly indicate the need for an attack against broad patterns of discrimination. Through the use of commissioner charges such an attack could be given priority; the agency could select major discriminators in each industry and region and initiate innovative litigation attacking the discriminatory employment systems of large enterprises. This approach, however, requires a comprehensive litigation strategy, with internal coordination throughout the agency. Such a strategy, essential to realizing the fundamental purposes of Title VII, never existed within the EEOC, and there is no reason to believe that a change will occur in the foreseeable future.[4]

The dismal record of the EEOC is surpassed by the ineffectiveness of the Office of Federal Contract Compliance Programs (OFCCP), which has the responsibility for enforcing federal executive orders prohibiting employment discrimination by government contractors. Since a very large part of the civilian economy is directly dependent upon government contracts, and virtually every major employer operates with such contracts, vigorous enforcement of the executive orders could have a significant impact on employment patterns throughout the nation.

The OFCCP has had little positive impact beyond eliminating a handful of the discriminatory practices they have chosen to attack. This record is especially significant given the agency's mandate and its power to cancel or withhold valuable government contracts. But the OFCCP has rarely invoked the federal contracting power against job discrimination, despite decisions by U.S. appellate courts that legally sanction such use.[5]

The office of Federal Contract Compliance Programs has failed to function as an enforcement agency. The conclusion reached by the U.S. Commission on Civil Rights in 1971 is an accurate description of the failure of enforcement during the past decade and is if anything more relevant today: "Although the order had important potential because of its sanctions, it did not bring about significant changes because its penalty provisions were never employed."[6] Unfortunately chapter 6 of the NRC report ignores this important record and its significance for many aspects of the study.

In the course of a brief and inadequate discussion of the racial practices of labor unions, consisting of a two-and-a-half-page digest based on a limited selection of published material (pp. 85-88), the report states that "the tradition of honoring seniority also made it difficult to improve black promotion opportunities because it effectively froze into place the discrimination that had previously existed" (p. 87). While noting the structural changes in the economy and the increasing elimination of jobs in manufacturing industries such as automobiles and steel, the unions in these industries, according to chapter 6 of the report, "had been particularly open to blacks" (p. 296).

While both statements taken separately are correct, the implications of the comment on page 87 conflict with the suggestion on page 296 regarding unions in manufacturing industries. Industrial unions whose origins are in the Congress of Industrial Organizations, in contrast to the racially exclusive craft unions of the American Federation of Labor, admitted black workers but engaged in a variety of discriminatory practices after blacks had been admitted. The forms of racial discrimination changed, but the substance did not, as industrial unions also functioned primarily to advance the interests of white workers, guaranteeing for them privileges in the labor market.

After Title VII of the Civil Rights Act went into effect, black workers who were members of industrial unions filed many charges with the Equal Employment Opportunity Commission. They initiated lawsuits in federal courts against labor organizations because they had learned that what racial exclusion was to the craft unions, segregated lines of job promotion and seniority were to the industrial unions. These issues have been the subject of extensive litigation under the Civil Rights Act.

Typical of many cases involving the United Steelworkers and other industrial unions was the decision of a federal court which found the union and the Bethlehem Steel Corporation in Lackawanna, New York, to be in violation of the law. The court stated that:

> The pervasiveness and longevity of the overt discriminatory hiring and job assignment practices, admitted by Bethlehem and the union, compel the conclusion that the present seniority and transfer provisions were based on past discriminatory classifications. . . . Job assignment practices were reprehensible. Over 80% of black workers were placed in eleven departments which contained the hotter and dirtier jobs in the plant. Blacks were excluded from higher paying and cleaner jobs.[7]

Observing that discriminatory contract provisions were embodied in nationwide labor agreements negotiated by the international union in 1962, 1965, and 1968, the court also stated that "The Lackawanna plant was a microcosm of classic job discrimination in the North, making clear why Congress enacted Title VII of the Civil Rights Act of 1964."[8]

It is significant that in the *Bethlehem Steel* case, the U.S. Court of Appeals for the Second Circuit stated that the job expectations of whites, based on union seniority practices, "arise from an illegal system. . . .Moreover, their seniority advantages are not indefeasibly vested rights but were expectations derived from a bargaining agreement subject to modification. . . ."[9]

Federal courts repeatedly found the Steelworkers Union guilty of violating Title VII, and in 1974 the union and major employers in steel manufacturing negotiated an industry-wide consent decree in an attempt to obtain an immunity from future lawsuits brought by black workers. But the effort to ward off further judicial intervention in the racial practices of the steel industry only partially succeeded, as litigation continued.[10]

In addition to the Steelworkers Union, many other industrial unions were defendants in employment discrimination cases under Title VII. Such litigation involved labor organizations in papermaking and communications, in the tobacco industry, in aircraft and automotive manufacturing (both the United Auto Workers and the International Association of Machinists), among longshoremen in public utilities, and in the transportation industry, among others.

The litigation record under Title VII involving the United Auto Workers is most relevant.[11] According to data presented in hearings of the U.S. Commission on Civil Rights in 1960, black workers during that period constituted seven-tenths of one percent of the skilled labor force in Detroit auto plants, while 42.3% of the laborers were black and 18.3% of production workers were black.[12]

A national survey by the U.S. Commission on Civil Rights, published in 1961, revealed that:

> In Detroit Negroes constituted a substantial portion–from 20 to 30 percent–of the total work force. [But] . . . their representation in "nontraditional" jobs was slight. . . . In Baltimore, each of the companies employed Negroes only in production work and not above the semiskilled level. . . .In Atlanta, the two automobile assembly plants contacted employed no Negroes in assembly operations. Except for one driver of an inside power truck, all Negro employees observed were engaged in janitorial work–sweeping, mopping, or carrying away trash.[13]

The report of the Negro American Labor Council, dated November 30, 1963, on the racial pattern in UAW plants in several cities provided further documentation and confirmed the conclusions of the commission. Quite clearly, the Skilled Trades Department of the UAW was continuing as a "lily white" enclave.

Based on the EEO-I Reports (Title VII requires every employer covered by the Civil Rights Act to file detailed reports on the composition and distribution of the employed labor force) the Equal Employment Opportunity Commission found that in 1975 black auto workers were still concentrated in lower level jobs and that the traditional racial pattern remained largely intact.[14] After more than 35 years of the UAW, this was the record in organized plants. In retrospect, it is evident that given the litigation record, industrial unions as well as craft unions tend to institutionalize the racial status quo, while the basic premise of contemporary civil rights laws and of black aspirations is that the racial status quo must be altered.[15]

In the first nine years after the Civil Rights Act went into effect, 1,335 Title VII charges were filed against the United Auto Workers, and throughout the 1970s and 1980s the UAW continued to be a defendant in Title VII litigation.[16]

The litigation record makes it very clear that in many different occupations, including a variety of public sector jobs, such as fire and police, whites held all the places on the seniority ladder precisely because blacks and other nonwhite workers were systematically excluded from competition for those jobs. Various union seniority systems were established at a time when racial minorities were barred from employment and union membership. Obviously blacks as a group, not just as individuals, constituted a class of victims who could not develop seniority status. A seniority system launched under these conditions inevitably becomes the institutionalized mechanism whereby whites as a group are granted racial privilege.

The failure to examine in a substantive manner these and other issues that are crucial to an understanding of the black economic condition is a major weakness of chapter 6 of the NRC report. Qualification of data, however elaborate, cannot compensate for this limited perspective, which has resulted in the report's regrettably superficial and inconclusive treatment of urgent racial problems.

References

1.   U.S. General Accounting Office. (1988, October). *Equal Employment Opportunity*. Washington, DC: Government Printing Office.

2.   In 1976, the U.S. General Accounting Office concluded: "In the aggregate, our analysis suggests that the EEOC has had little impact on alleviating problems of systemic employment discrimination. Comparisons of nationwide employment statistics, as well as analysis of data for employers under conciliation agreements, show little change over the years in the employment status of minorities and women." U.S. General Accounting Office. (1976). *The EEOC Has Made Limited Progress in Eliminating Employment Discrimination*. Washington, DC: Government Printing Office. Pp. 38-39.

3.   *Burlington Northern, Inc., v. Equal Employment Opportunity Commission*, 644 F. 2d 717, 25 FEP Cases 499 8th Cir. 1981. See also *Equal Employment Opportunity Commission v. Jos. Horne, Co.*, 607 F. 2d 1075, 20 FEP Cases 1752 (4th Cir. 1979).

4.   For a detailed critical analysis of the EEOC together with recommendations, see Hill, H. (1983, Winter). The Equal Employment Opportunity Commission: Twenty Years Later. *The Journal of Intergroup Relations, 11* (4), 45-72. This essay was based on the author's testimony before the Subcommittee on Employment Opportunities, Committee on Education and Labor, U.S. House of Representatives, Washington, D.C., October 26, 1983.

5.   See for example *Contractors Association of Eastern Pennsylvania v. Schultz*, 442 F. 2d 159 (3rd Cir. 1971), cert denied, and *Builders Association v. Ogilvie*, 471 F. 2d 680 (7th Cir. 1972). See also *Chrapliwy v. Uniroyal Inc.*, 670 F. 2d 760, 28 FEP 19 (7th Cir. 1982).

6.   U.S. Commission on Civil Rights. (1971). *Federal Civil Rights Enforcement Effort*. Washington, DC: Government Printing Office. P. 46. There is an extensive critical literature on this subject. See, for example: U.S. General Accounting Office. (1975). *The Equal Employment Opportunity Program for Federal Non-Construction Contractors Can Be Improved*. Washington, DC: Government Printing Office. See also: Washington, S.W. & Faughran, W.D. (1979, September). The Old Compliance Ball Game and the New. *The Journal of Intergroup Relations*, 4-15.

7.   *United States v. Bethlehem Steel Corp.*, 446 F. 2d 652, 3 FEP 589 (2nd Cir. 1971).

8.   Ibid. P. 655.

9.   Ibid. P. 663.

10.   An example of recent litigation on these issues that continued into 1988 is the class action discrimination suit against the Steelworkers Union and the Lukens Steel Co. of Coatesville, PA. The U.S. Court of Appeals for the Third Circuit found that the union had violated both Title VII and the Civil Rights Act of 1964 by failing in "the affirmative duty . . . to combat discrimination in the workplace" by not processing grievances involving race. *Goodman v. Lukens Steel Co. and United Steelworkers of America, AFL-CIO*, 777 F. 2d 113 (3rd Cir. 1985).

11.   Other unions with "liberal" reputations were also named as defendants in Title VII litigation. Among these were the International Ladies Garment Workers Union. Many complaints were filed by nonwhite and female workers against the union with the EEOC, and in some of these cases the commission sustained charges of race and sex discrimination by the ILGWU and entered a verdict of guilty against the parent international union as well as its local affiliate. *Violetta Puttermann v. Knitgoods Workers Union Local 155 of ILGWU, International Ladies Garment Workers Union, Sol Greene and Sol C. Chaiken*, U.S. District Court, Southern District of New York. Memorandum Opinion and Order, 78 Civ. 6000 (MJL), August 20, 1983. Among the many EEOC charges against the ILGWU were cases in New York, Chicago, Philadelphia, Cleveland, Atlanta, and other cities.

12.   U.S. Commission on Civil Rights. (1961). *Hearing Before the U.S. Commission on Civil Rights, Detroit, Michigan, December 14-15, 1960*. Washington, DC: Government Printing Office.

13.   U.S. Commission on Civil Rights. (1961). *Employment*. Report No. 3. Washington, DC: Government Printing Office. P. 65.

14.   Employment Analysis Report Program, U.S. Equal Employment Opportunity Commission. (1975). *1975 EEO-I Report Summary by Industry Within SMSA's Detroit, Michigan*. Washington, DC: Government Printing Office.

15.   Analysis of the litigation record under Title VII reveals much of significance and confirms this observation. In *Aikens v. U.S. Postal Service*, for example, a case argued before the U.S. Supreme Court in 1983, the AFL-CIO joined with the Chamber of Commerce and the Reagan Justice Department in attacking the rights of minority workers under Title VII. The labor federation argued for new stringent standards of proof that would make it more difficult for workers to prove that they were the victims of racial discrimination. Although no unions were involved in this case, the AFL-CIO sought to undermine the position of black workers seeking legal remedies for job discrimination. (665 F. 2d 1057, 26 FEP 1151 [1981], cert granted, 455 U.S. 1015 [1982].) The brief amicus curiae filed by the AFL-CIO in *Boston Firefight-*

ers Union v. Boston Chapter NAACP and in other cases, argued for the elimination of affirmative action remedies.

16.   United Automobile Workers. (1976, May). *Twenty-Seven Years of Civil Rights.* UAW Constitutional Convention Reports, 1947-1974, International Union. Detroit, MI: Author. See also: Hill, H. (1985). *Black Labor and the American Legal System.* Madison, WI: University of Wisconsin Press. Pp. 260-270.

Herbert Hill is a professor of Afro-American studies and industrial relations at the University of Wisconsin-Madison.

Critique of Chapter 7,
"The Schooling of Black Americans"

Antoine M. Garibaldi
with the Study Group on Education

The chapter on education in the National Research Council's study (Chapter 7: "The Schooling of Black Americans") does an excellent job of assembling and synthesizing a variety of research studies to assess the current educational performance of black Americans. While it is true that many more blacks are obtaining an elementary and secondary education in the 1980s than in the 1940s, the data also clearly shows that substantial gaps remain between whites and blacks with respect to educational performance at all levels of the educational continuum. However, the chapter is less than definitive because of its failure to acknowledge some of the critical reasons for this discrepancy and because of its failure to recommend actions that could reverse these negative trends.

The chapter indicates that there are still large numbers of black students who have not completed high school (at least one-fourth of black adults); they are twice as likely as whites not to graduate from high school. The proportion of black high school graduates who have gone on to college has declined steadily since the mid-1970 peak years of black enrollment (48% of black high school graduates in 1977 went to college compared to 36.5% in 1986); and while the percentage of blacks who had completed college in 1980 (approximately 11.5%) was five times greater than the percentage of blacks who had completed college in 1940, blacks' annual undergraduate degree representation is still only about 6%. There has also been a significant decline in graduate school attendance; and blacks' annual doctoral representation is less than 4%. All this, along with the shrinking proportion of black teachers, portrays a discouraging future for blacks at all levels of education. The National Research Council (NRC) chapter ignores a huge body of scholarly research over the past 15 years, conducted largely by black researchers, which demonstrates that the presence of black teachers at all levels of education substantially affects black students' enrollment, matriculation, and graduation.

In assessing the magnitude of the educational progress of black Americans over the last 50 years, the judgment is definitely mixed. Even though few will question that gains have been made in educational attainment, careful assessments demonstrate that the deviation between black and white attainment is still significantly large. Surprisingly, the authors of the NRC chapter have failed to provide any historical context for improvements in educational access and attainment (e.g., open admissions policies, the Adams case, positive benefits of desegregation in urban areas, etc.). Though improvements have produce marginal results, many disadvantaged urban and rural black children continue to fare poorly on achievement tests and assessments of fundamental literacy skills, large numbers continue to drop out of schools early in their secondary school years, and still more are being relegated to classes for remedial and special education instruction–labels that students carry with them throughout the remainder of their school years.

Enrollment in public schools in most urban areas is already mostly nonwhite (primarily black and Hispanic American), and scores on standardized tests of achievement and aptitude demonstrate that their performance is far from the national mean. It is important to note that in 1989 blacks scored approximately five points below the national mean on the ACT (13.6 compared to 18.8) and an average of 75 points lower on the verbal and mathematics sections of the SAT. (There have been slight, fluctuating improvements for blacks on these measures over the last couple of years.) Thus, just as in the observed gains on the reading, mathematics, and science tests of the National Assessment of Educational Progress, assessments of black students' "educational progress" must be qualified and results must be interpreted with great care. The apparent gains require qualitative interpretation. Are we succeeding or failing? Is the "cup" of educational progress "half-empty" or "half-full"?

Schools modeling their education programs after the characteristics and the tenets of the "effective schools" research, for example, have produced significant increases in student performance. But the fact remains that very small cohorts of nonwhite and disadvantaged youth are benefiting from these successful strategies. As for the magnet schools white students and nonwhite students from a high socioeconomic strata generally make up the mix. More must be done to make it possible for less advantaged groups of students in urban schools to participate in these programs. Similarly, proven programs such as Headstart and Chapter 1 deserve more funding from federal and state funds to help the large number of nonwhite students who enter school without adequate preschool preparation to succeed.

It is surprising that the NRC treatment of school desegregation (which the authors describe as an "overarching" event) receives only a page and a half of discussion. Similarly, the authors have ignored the importance of intra-district inequalities of resources. In the largest scale investigation of whether "equivalent resources for the education of all students" were provide to black, Hispanic, and female students in the New York City public schools, the United States Office for Civil Rights found sweeping deficiencies and inequalities in materials, services, and facilities. Differences in budget allocation between so-called "minority" and "majority" schools were overwhelmingly obvious and were found even between classrooms in the same school. Such differences with respect to allocations per student must be viewed as deliberate and should be considered when discussing the 1966 Coleman, Campbell, et al. study. There is need, too, for consideration of classes that are not offered at many urban schools attended by blacks. Ogbu's study in Stockton, California, demonstrates, though it is not described in the NRC chapter, how organized black parents can force schools to provide the same science classes offered at predominantly white schools and how well black students can perform in them. Unequal resources significantly affect achievement and must always be considered in evaluating educational progress.

It is also important to recognize that the authors posit the notion (p. 354) that a possible cause of black/white differences in educational achievement is "differences in ability." This dangerous inference revives the hotly debated "theoretical" argument of genetic influences on achievement. The suggestion of differences in group ability is countered by several studies in the same chapter that provide strong evidence against innate group differences and point to external factors, as well as internal school variables, as the primary indicators of differential academic performance. The value of genes in the "nature-nurture" argument holds even less weight today because many studies–of Asian-Americans as well as African-Americans–convincingly show that effort and family expectations, rather than innate ability, most significantly contribute to academic success and achievement.

With respect to college entrance and degree attainment of blacks, historically black colleges have been responsible for graduating disproportionate amounts of black degree recipients, even though they represent less than 5% of all institutions of higher education. However, their resources and facilities are so limited that they cannot accommodate greater numbers of students. The nation's other 3,400 institutions need to recruit and graduate more black and other nonwhite students; the proportion of black students in two-year colleges must also be increased.

One key area where the NRC study hedges is on the impact that decreases in financial aid have had on the decline in college-going rates of blacks. While the chapter states that outright grants, as a percentage of all financial aid, have declined from 80% to 46% between 1975-76 and 1985-86, and that loans have increased from 17% to 50% during this same period, the conclusion states, "We cannot conclude with certainty that the cause [of the declining number of black high school graduates attending college] has been the significant decline in (real) financial aid grants to students...." (p. 379) Reductions in financial aid have unequivocally had an impact on the number of black students entering college in recent years, as have tuition increases at state as well as private institutions over the last decade.[1]

To achieve realistic gains in educational progress for black Americans in the next decade and in the next century, it is critically important that more financial aid be provided so that their reliance on loans is minimized. Increases in undergraduate tuition grants will also increase the probability that these young people will pursue graduate and professional school. In secondary schools, more counselors are needed to increase the amount and quality of advising that students receive so that they will be properly guided toward available postsecondary opportunities. The latter might be accomplished through block grants provided by the federal government to local education agencies. Similarly, increased aid from the government is necessary to replicate the successes of programs such as Headstart and Chapter 1. There is much to be done from preschool to graduate and professional schools if black Americans are to substantially improve their educational status in this country.

References

1.   According to a 1982 study by the College Board entitled *Profiles: College Bound Seniors, 1981* (published by the College Entrance and Examination Board, New York), in 1981 almost half of the black seniors planning to enter college came from families with incomes less than $12,000, compared to only 10% of white seniors. A 1987 study by the United Negro College Fund and National Institute of Independent Colleges and Universities entitled *Access to College: The Impact of Federal Financial Aid Policies at Private Historically Black Colleges* (published by UNCF, New York and NICU, Washington, DC) demonstrated that federal grants accounted for 53% of all financial aid to students at the 43 private black colleges of the UNCF in 1979-80, but federal grants to students at these same institutions accounted for only 37% of their financial aid. Given the fact that the median family income of students at UNCF schools is $11,000, the majority of these students would certainly not be able to finance their education without educational grants from federal sources.

Antoine Garibaldi is dean of the College of Arts and Sciences at Xavier University in New Orleans.

Critique of Chapter 8,
"Black Americans' Health"

William A. Darity, Sr.

General Concerns

The health and the social status of black Americans have remained at a very low level since blacks arrived on the shores of the New World before 1619. In addressing the issue of health the National Research Council's (NRC) report points out that there has been improvement in the health of black Americans. This is true. But what the report does not point out is that there has been improvement in the health of *all* Americans. To make this improvement appear to be a benefit to black Americans is to be disingenuously protective of a socioeconomic and political system that continues to discriminate, in the area of health among many other areas, against blacks.

The improvement of health in this country has not been consistent across the board. This inconsistency was called to our attention over 25 years ago by the late Whitney Young, the executive director of the National Urban League, and by Paul Cornely, former president of the American Public Health Association.[1] What has actually happened is that there have been improvements in some selected health variables for all members of the United States population, but the issue is for which group is there a greater improvement. Data demonstrate there is a widening of the gap between white and black Americans.

In order to address this issue, some years ago I developed a measure called the differential deficit ratio (DDR)–a procedure that helps us to see this gap and to explain the disparities.[2] For example, when you look at the trend line in figure 1 you will see that it shows a drop in infant mortality for blacks and whites. In 1950 the infant mortality rate for whites was 26.8 and for blacks it was 43.9. The DDR illustrates that in 1950 the DDR was 63.8% and in 1975 the DDR was 84.5%. (See table 1.) And the DDR continued to increase until 1980 when it dropped to 74.4%, but by 1985 it had increased to 95.6%. The NRC report did not employ such an analyses. The omission was critical. In fact, no clear analytical procedure was employed by the NRC.

Other health problems that the report addresses were heart disease, diabetes, and some of the cerebral vascular diseases. Again the report did not address the issues from an analytical point of view. Let us examine the rates of chronic diseases of the liver and cirrhosis. The DDR was -17.2 when the rate for black males was 8.8/100,000 and for white males 11.6/100,000 in 1950. In other words, the rate of chronic liver disease and cirrhosis was higher in whites than it was in blacks. By 1985, the DDR was 85.7%; the rate was 23.4/100,000 for black males and 12.6/100,000 for white males.[3] What the DDR emphasizes is that blacks are losing ground. We need to consider special efforts and programs addressed specifically to black Americans.

The report usefully presents concrete facts on the differential rates in illness, disabilities, and deaths. It stresses the fact that not *all* black Americans are unhealthy. But it says it in so righteous and condescending a way that we may appropriately wonder for whom this report was written? Was it intended for the helping professions or was it politically motivated?

The report addresses the issue of maternal and child health simplistically: In pregnancy we need to identify and carry out health education. Next, insure that all pregnant women, especially those at medical and social economic risks, are given access to and receive high quality care. This is all well and good, but the real issue is how to implement and administer–and fund–such a program. Another superficial recommendation is a public information program about low-weight babies. What we need to do is address some of the real issues: poverty, unemployment, lack of skills, lack of health insurance, discrimination, and segregation.

The report gives information on malnutrition, anemia, lead poisoning, lack of immunization, dental care, child neglect and abuse, and teenage child-bearing. At one point it is stated that in addition to risk of pregnancy, early onset of unprotected intercourse among blacks placed them at a higher risk of contracting sexually transmitted diseases. The statement implies that a woman who uses a diaphragm or pills to prevent pregnancy will be protected from sexually transmitted diseases. This, of course, is not at all true. The chapter on health leaves much to be desired.

The report also addresses health careers. The proportion of blacks per 100,000 population in health careers is the lowest of any of the racial/ethnic groups in the United States. For Asians there are approximately 1,400 physicians per 100,000 Asian population; for whites, there are approximately 200; and for blacks, approximately 50.[4] The report undertook no comparative analysis so that one might begin to trace the effects of discrimination. Despite these reservations, I consider this to be the best section of the chapter.

I believe we can solve our health problems if our government has the will. Let's use infant mortality as an example. In 1950 the infant mortality rate for Native Americans was 82.1 per 1,000 live births, for blacks it was 43.9, and for whites it was 26.8. In 1983, the rate for whites had dropped to 9.7, for blacks to 19.2, for Native Americans to 10.7. If you look at the infant mortality rate now among whites, blacks, Native Americans, Chinese, Japanese, and other Americans, blacks have the highest infant mortality rate. (See table 2.) The infant mortality rate is critical since it is the index used to determine the overall status of the family and group.[5] If we use infant mortality as a simple index, we can say that blacks rate lowest amongst all the racial/ethnic groups in this country. Most of the decrease in infant mortality between 1950 and 1970 among other nonwhites has been the result of a crash health program among Native Americans, which demonstrates the capability of the federal government to further equity when it wishes to do so.

Specific Concerns

It is my belief that our system of health care needs to undergo organizational changes to eliminate favoritism towards the health care profession itself and towards the wealthy. We need to establish a program of national health insurance, and we need to move towards a comprehensive national health service. It is my opinion that all professionals in the health care system should be salaried and should be monitored and evaluated annually just as we in the universities are. I do not see why patients should have a selected provider for health care. They should select a system. What is wrong with the present system is that it operates to benefit the professional rather than the client. It is based on reward for taking care of the ill and little or no reward for keeping people well. The system should reward physicians and health professionals for keeping people well–preventive health care.

The public and health care professionals alike should be reeducated towards a new concept of health. We need to get people to realize that health care is a right and that it is a public and social responsibility. Education is not a private responsibility. Why should health care be a private responsibility?

Special Effort

A special developmental effort is required to deal with the health of the black population. As the poverty level rises there is an impact on unemployment, on housing, on education, and on health, most dramatically indicated in infant mortality. Unfortunately, many officials in the federal administration are talking about the private domain and voluntarism. Over the years the federal government supported discriminatory laws and segregation, and it is therefore a major responsibility of the federal government to solve the problem that it helped to create. It is recommended that municipalities, metropolitan areas, local governments, towns, counties, states, and the federal government establish special task forces and programs to deal with the health problems of black Americans.

For example, we must be more specific in addressing problems that relate to blacks and not use "minority" as a cliche or a mode of reference. With that model we may miss our target. Educators, health workers, social workers, agriculture workers, and labor organizations are all going to have to work together in finding solutions.

Since health care is a social problem, it is also a political problem. We must remove health care from the cloak of secrecy of the doctor/patient relationship. Consumer groups, in particular minority consumer groups, must be trained to access health statistics and epidemiological findings and use them in the political process. This will put pressure on federal, state, and congressional delegations to place emphasis on the development of health care programs that will meet the needs of individual black Americans, black families, and the black community.

It is my opinion that political leaders should be responsible for their constituency's health and health care. To support them in this effort we need to initiate and start pressing for class-action suits to enforce responsibility for implementation of programs. We need to work with groups and organizations like the NAACP Legal Defense and Education Fund and the Urban League to bring legal suits against municipalities, town, and states. As a beginning what we need to do is get a few cases on the docket. This will get the politicians thinking more about the problems. We must put all our resources together and do something meaningful for the entire black population.

I hope that in future studies the sponsoring group will establish guidelines that will define the problem by analyzing comparative aspects. In so doing the real issues can be addressed and recommendations can be made towards the development of genuine parity in health care.

Figure 1

Infant Mortality Rate (IMR) for Whites and Blacks, and
Differential Deficit Ratio (DDR) United States, 1950 through 1985

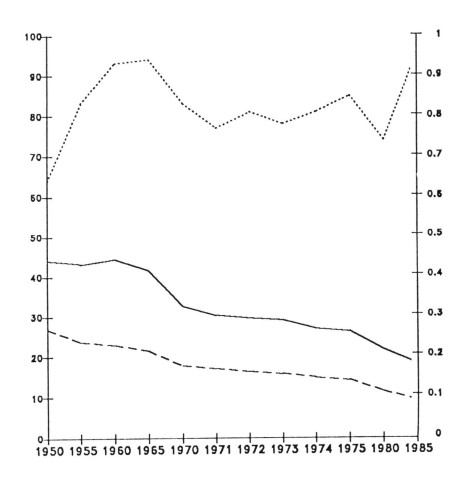

	1950	1955	1960	1965	1970	1975	1980	1985
IMR								
Blacks	43.9	43.1	44.3	41.7	32.6	26.2	21.4	18.2
Whites	26.8	23.6	22.9	21.5	17.8	14.2	11.4	-9.3
DDR	64%	83%	93%	94%	83%	85%	74%	96%

Table 1

Comparison of Infant Mortality Rates and Differential Deficit Ratio
(DDR) for Blacks and Whites, in the United States, 1950-1985

Year	All Races	White	All Other	Black	Difference Black & White	Differential Deficit Ratio
1950	29.2	26.8	44.5	43.9	17.1	.638 or 63.8%
1955	26.4	23.6	42.8	43.1	19.5	.826 or 82.6%
1960	26.0	22.9	43.2	44.3	21.4	.934 or 93.4%
1965	24.7	21.5	40.3	41.7	20.2	.940 or 94.0%
1970	20.0	17.8	30.9	32.6	14.8	.831 or 83.1%
1971	19.1	17.1	28.5	30.3	13.2	.772 or 77.2%
1972	18.5	16.4	27.2	29.6	13.2	.805 or 80.5%
1973	17.7	15.8	26.2	28.1	12.3	.778 or 77.8%
1974	16.7	14.8	24.9	26.8	12.0	.881 or 81.1%
1975	16.1	14.2	24.2	26.2	12.0	.845 or 84.5%
1980	12.5	11.4	19.1	21.8	11.4	.744 or 74.4%
1985	10.6	9.3	15.8	18.4	9.3	.956 or 95.6%

Sources: *Health – United States*, 1982, U.S. Dept. of Health and Human Services,
p. 9. *N.Y. Times*, January 8, 1984, p. 41 and *Boston Globe*, January 8,
1984, p. 2. *Health Status of the Disadvantaged, Chartbook*, 1986, U.S. Dept.
of Health and Human Services, Publication No. (HRSA) HRS-P-DV86-2, p.
29. DDR calculated by presenter. *Statistical Abstracts of the United States*,
1988, (108th Edition) U.S. Dept. of Commerce/Bureau of Census, p. 75.

Table 2

Infant Mortality Rates Specified by Race,
United States, 1950-1983
(Rate per 1000 live births)

Year and Percentages	All Races	White	Black	Native Americans	Chinese	Japanese	Other Races
1950	29.2	26.8	43.9	82.1	19.3	19.1	27.9
1955	26.4	23.6	43.1	59.7	18.1	10.9	17.6
1960	26.0	22.9	44.3	49.3	14.7	15.3	23.5
1965	24.7	21.5	41.7	NA	9.0	10.0	NA
1970	20.0	17.8	32.7	22.0	8.4	10.5	14.8
1975	16.1	14.2	26.1	17.8	4.4	6.9	9.8
1978	13.8	12.0	23.1	13.7	6.3	6.5	8.5
1980	12.6	11.0	21.4	13.2	5.3	4.5	2.8
1983	11.6	9.7	19.2	10.7	6.5	4.3	3.0

Percentage Decrease

1950-1978	112%	123%	90.4%	499%	206%	193%	228%
1950-1983	152%	176%	128%	667%	197%	344%	830%

Sources: *The Disadvantaged, Chartbook*, 1977, U.S. Dept. of Health and Human Services, Publication No. (HRA) 77-678. *Health of Minorities and Women, Chartbook*, 1982, American Public Health Association, p. 35. *Health Status of the Disadvantaged, Chartbook*, 1986, U.S. Dept. of Health and Human Services, Publication No. (HRSA) HRS-P-DV86-2.

References

1.   Young, W. (1964). *Health Care and the Negro Population*. New York: National Urban League. Cornelly, P. (1969, April). "The Health Status of the Negro Today and in the Future." *American Journal of Public Health, 58* (4), 647-654.

2.   Darity, W.A. (1987). Socio-Economic Factors Influencing the Health Status of Black Americans. *International Journal of Community Health Education, 7* (2), 91-108.

3.   Ibid. Department of Health and Human Services. (1988, March). *Health Status and Determinants 1987*. Washington, DC: Government Printing Office.

4.   Director, Office of Data Analysis and Management. (1983, March 23). Memo from Director, BH PR: 1980, Census Estimate for Health Occupations. Washington, DC: Government Printing Office.

5.   Darity, W.A. (1988). The Widening Disparity in Health Status of Black and White Americans: A Comparative Analysis. Paper presented at the National Invitational Conference, National Center for the Advancement of Blacks in the Health Professions, Detroit, Michigan, December 16-17, 1988. Revised and presented at the first Annual William A. Hinton Lecture at the Harvard School of Public Health, February 8, 1989. Further revised and presented at the Distinguished Faculty Lecture Series, University of Massachusetts at Amherst, March 2, 1989 (unpublished).

William A. Darity, Sr., is a professor of public health in the School of Public Health, University of Massachusetts at Amherst.

Critique of Chapter 9,
"Crime and the Administration of Criminal Justice"

E. Yvonne Moss

The summary of the National Research Council's (NRC) report on crime and criminal justice begins with the observation that there is widespread distrust among black Americans of the criminal justice system. The reasons are obvious from the report. Racial discrimination has been documented at various times and places. Black Americans are overrepresented as victims and defendants. Black people are twice as likely as whites to be victims of robbery, vehicle theft, and aggravated assault. Homicide claims the life of black victims six to seven times more often than whites. Concomitantly, black victims incur greater monetary and medical costs and more time loss from work than white victims. The gap in arrests rates between blacks and whites is widening, while the percentage of black Americans among the nation's prison population has increased to 47%.

Yet the study concludes that racial bias in the criminal justice system cannot be determined even though a "conclusion that discrimination against blacks...is absent is not justified...[by] current data."[1] The apparently contradictory findings of the report highlight the basic failure of the study: the attempt to explain away racial discrimination as insignificant or unimportant.

The NRC report reinforces the five-to-four decision in *McCleskey*.[2] The court acknowledged that disparity was proven in the imposition of the death penalty. Nevertheless, by a one-vote majority the court ruled that:

> such discrepancies do not violate the Equal Protection Clause of the Fourteenth Amendment. In order to prevail under that Clause, a criminal defendant (unlike an employment discrimination plaintiff, for example) must prove that decisionmakers in his case acted with discriminatory purpose.[3]

Reminiscent of *Plessy's* 1896 legal justification of segregation, the *McCleskey* ruling provides a legal justification for the discriminatory application of the death penalty. Execution is the ultimate penalty in any society. Giving legal sanction to discrimination in capital punishment makes a mockery of the ideal of equal justice under law.

Central to the NRC report's conclusion that racial bias cannot be determined is the controversy within the scholarly community over empirical evidence of disparity. Given the context of criminal justice administration in the United States, it is not surprising that empirical studies do not conclude definitively whether or not a charge of racial bias can universally be applied. There are 51 "systems" of criminal justice in the United States: one federal system and 50 state systems. In each state there is great variety in structure, budgetary responsibility, and local autonomy. Traditionally, in American society, the law enforcement and adjudication functions have been highly decentralized. Judges, prosecutors, and parole officials, key actors in criminal processing, have enormous discretion in the exercise of their authority.

The historical ubiquity of discrimination against blacks in arrests and sentencing is acknowledged by the NRC summary. Yet, the historical absence of a legal standard dictating equal treatment under law is ignored. It has only been 35 years since the Supreme Court ruled in *Brown*[4] that black Americans were entitled to equal protection of the law. This "seachange" in legal tradition, along with reform in court administration, corrections, and sentencing over the last 20 years, has contributed to the difficulties in assessing racial bias.

Even so, to dismiss findings of discrimination in some jurisdictions or some aspects of criminal justice processing because uncontroversial, universally applicable, aggregate data analysis is unavailable is, from the perspective of public policy, irresponsible. The question is not whether a uniform indictment or clean bill of health can be given to American justice on the issue of racial discrimination. The really important question is whether racial (or gender or status) discrimination is acceptable in any jurisdiction or in any aspect of the process when it is uncovered by reputable, credible studies. When these studies uncover patterns of bias in the administration of justice, are those patterns of bias and the resulting racial disadvantage acceptable in our society and under our legal values?

If we take the ideals of due process and equal justice under the law seriously, the responsible answer is no. Effective social control requires respect for law as well as tough law enforcement. Respect for law is not possible if punishment is distributed by race or status and if persons are punished not for the crimes they commit but for extralegal factors that are illegitimate to the process.

One aspect of racial discrimination in the administration of justice that deserves special comment is the leniency towards assailants whose victims are black. Such leniency, whether in felonies or less serious crimes, sends a disturbing message: that black life and property are not worth protecting to the degree that we protect white life and property. This type of racial bias, along with differential treatment of defendants and offenders, is not acceptable in a system of justice that strives both symbolically and substantively for fair and impartial treatment of accused persons and fair and effective punishment for offenders.

The attempt to deny the significance of racial bias along with the contradictory nature of the findings constitute the two major problems with the NRC report. Another is the problem of perspective, i.e., from whose eyes and with regard to whose interests are the issues of crime and criminal justice evaluated? The NRC report does not consider the perspectives or needs of black citizens, which are vital in this area. For example, the local criminal justice function is traditionally conceived of strictly in terms of crime control. The crime control model includes a presumption of guilt while the tasks of criminal justice agencies are limited to apprehension, arrest, sentencing, and warehousing offenders. This model is inadequate to meet the needs of black citizens for a number of reasons.

Most victims of crime are black and economically among the near-poor. Most crime is intraracial, that is, committed against persons of one's own race. Most crime takes place near an offender's home. Estimates are that only half of all crimes committed ever get reported. Less than 20% of crimes committed result in arrests. About 10% are arraigned on warrant. Only 8% of all crime results in conviction. Half of those in prison are black. Ninety-five percent of those in prison will eventually be released back into society. And, the recidivism rate remains high. These considerations necessitate a broader concept and a different approach to the administration of justice than the crime control model allows.

A due process model that insists on a guarantee of procedural fairness should be taken seriously. This, however, represents only a first step. A criminal justice system that adequately serves the needs of black Americans needs to do more. Chief Justice Samuel Gardner of Detroit's Recorder's Courts advises that while many convicted felons are criminals "pure and simple and we have no alternative but to lock them up....Still criminals can be made as well as punished by the criminal justice system, especially prison. It is our responsibility...to salvage everyone we can...."[5]

Action taken against lawbreakers should have three purposes beyond punishment: (1) removing dangerous people from the community; (2) deterring others from criminal behavior; and, (3) giving society an opportunity to attempt to transform lawbreakers into law-abiding citizens.[6] The traditional approach of simply warehousing criminals is not enough. Programs that rehabilitate and reconcile offenders to acceptable levels of community conduct are necessary.

Consider the following. The United States has the highest incarceration rate in the Western world. This creates tremendous fiscal as well as warehousing problems. In 1978 our country spent over $4 billion to construct and operate over 500 prisons with 400 in the planning stage. Some states spend as much as 500% more on prisons than on parole and probation. In 1978 each jail cell cost $50,000 to construct. Estimates ranged from $15,000 to $20,000 per year to keep a person imprisoned. For local communities the policy options are simply: Do we want to spend $50,000 per year on a jail cell or on housing? Do we want to spend $15,000 to $20,000 per year to warehouse a prisoner who is very likely to go back out on the streets and commit other crimes or do we want to develop and educate young people? Gardner characterizes many of these offenders as:

> young, functionally illiterate, and unemployed. They are not concerned with the future because they have none, as we know it, and contrary to a theory now widely being propounded, the prospect of punishment for their crimes neither occurs to them nor frightens them. Crime is a means of survival, providing a better living than any alternative currently available to them.[7]

Additionally problems arise with youth offenders and drugs. An incident from research on Detroit courts illustrates the point.[8] While examining homicide files I repeatedly came across the organization "Young Men Inc." It sounded like an upstanding social agency engaged in the process of moral uplift. Further investigation indicated that, on the contrary, this organization was the brain child of two enterprising young drug dealers who recruited youngsters for various jobs related to drug trafficking because criminal authorities had few options for handling very young offenders. Youngsters–eight, nine, ten years old and up–were paid anywhere from $200 or $300 to $1,000 a week to do various jobs. Some parents looked the other way when they learned of their children's involvement because the children brought home more money than the parents; and, the families needed the income. The dilemma is obvious: how do you tell a youngster to work hard so that when he grows up he can become a plumber and make perhaps $400 per week, when he has become accustomed to bringing home that much or more? Clearly more than a crime control approach is needed to address the issues of crime, values, and money. This brings us back to the question of values–what and how they are taught to our young–and the need for better social supports for families.

The National Research Council's report in its summary cites the dissatisfaction among black Americans with the criminal justice system as potentially a specific source of social turbulence. This dissatisfaction does not imply that black Americans are "soft on crime." On the contrary, studies of black attitudes on crime and the police reveal that black citizens want fair, effective, "tough" law-enforcement. What promotes dissatisfaction is dual victimization as defendants and as victims, along with harassment and disrespect for law-abiding citizens and even for court personnel who are black because of presumptions about black criminality.

Any serious treatment of the relationship of black Americans and the criminal justice systems should courageously confront evidence of racial discrimination and disadvantage where it is uncovered and recommend appropriate policies and remedies. Concern for the problems of crime and criminal justice should go beyond punishment to consider prevention, rehabilitation, and reconciliation of offenders. The functions of the criminal justice system should be conceptualized in broader terms than apprehension and warehousing. The purpose of the system should also be to include individual and community protection, regardless of race or social status. If the problems of crime are to be effectively addressed in terms of the larger society, striving for a system of justice that can gain the respect and trust of black Americans is imperative.

References

1.   Jaynes, G.D. & Williams, R.W., Jr., (Eds.) (1989). *A Common Destiny: Blacks and American Society.* Washington, DC: National Academy Press. P. 487.

2.   *McCleskey v. Kemp*, 481 U.S. 279 (1987); also see 107 S.Ct. 1756 (1987).

3.   Ibid.

4.   *Brown v. Board of Education, Topeka, Kansas*, 347 U.S. 483 (1954); 98L Ed. 873; 74 S.Ct. 686.

5.   Gardner, S. (1978, March 22). Remarks to monthly community crime prevention meeting. Detroit, MI.

6.   Gardner, S. (1978, January). Address to the graduating class at the Police Academy. Detroit, MI.

7.   Gardner, S. (1977, November 28). Letter to the Editor. *Detroit News.*

8.   Moss, E.Y. (1989). The Politics of Judicial Reform in Detroit. Ph.D. dissertation, Atlanta University.

E. Yvonne Moss is a research scientist for the William Monroe Trotter Institute at the University of Massachusetts at Boston.

Critique of Chapters 6 and 10, "Blacks in the Economy" and "Children and Families"

Robert B. Hill
and
James B. Stewart

Since the primary focus of the National Research Council (NRC) study was on changes in the social and economic status of blacks as individuals, black families were treated as a peripheral concern. In only two of its ten chapters was there any substantial discussion of family patterns: economic trends in black families were examined in chapter 6 ("Blacks in the Economy") and social trends among black families were examined in the final chapter ("Children and Families"). This critique will deal with the NRC's analysis of African-American families in these two chapters.

Overall, the NRC study reaffirms many reports on African-American families by organizations such as the U.S. Census Bureau, the National Urban League, the Children's Defense Fund, the Joint Center for Political Studies, and others. The NRC report concludes that while African-American families made unprecedented progress from the 1940s through the 1960s, these gains were markedly eroded during the 1970s and 1980s. Moreover, it rejects strongly the popular belief that welfare benefits were mainly responsible for the growth in female-headed black families and that a "culture of poverty" with distinctive values, beliefs, and behavior exists among low-income blacks.

Economic Trends

The NRC report presents several insightful findings about African-American families, although the presentation is often done in a superficial manner. One of the study's findings is that, contrary to conventional wisdom, the rise in single-parent families was not responsible for the increase in black poverty during the 1970s. As with other family types, the odds of being in poverty declines for black female-headed families. On the other hand, since the 1960s there has been a substantial decline in employment among black men, and this employment loss is a more important factor than the fact that female-headed families are more susceptible to poverty. Thus, the study reported that had black family structure in 1986 remained the same as in 1973, the percentage of poor black children would have fallen from 41% to 38% instead of rising to 43%. Thus the study concluded that low earnings of black men was more significant than family structure as a determinant of poverty: "Many intact black families are poor because two adults heading them have very low earning capacities. Likewise, many single-parent families would remain poor if there were two adults present" (pp. 281-282).

Furthermore, in table 6-2 of the NRC report, the data demonstrates that although black couples in which the woman works have median family incomes that are 82% of comparable white couples, black couples in which the woman does not work have incomes only 63% of comparable white couples. This underscores the disproportionate contribution of working women to the economic viability of two-parent African-American families. The NRC study proceeds to focus, appropriately enough, on the employment problems of black men, but it fails to also elaborate on the employment and earnings problems of black wives and black women heading families.

Another important finding that was treated superficially was the fact that, despite the record rise in black female-headed families, black reliance on public assistance did not increase, but remained at a constant 7.5% of total black family income since 1970 (only 23% of blacks received welfare in 1984).

The study devotes but two paragraphs to the problems of the working poor–in which no data for blacks is separately presented.

On the other hand, the NRC report makes a laudable attempt to provide a balanced treatment of the black middle class. It acknowledges that the gap between low-income and middle-income black families has widened since the 1960s and that the proportion of middle-income black families has leveled off during the same period. Moreover, it underscores the continuing economic gap between middle-class blacks and whites, whether income or wealth are used as criteria.

The limitations of treating families as only collections of individuals can be seen in the discussion of differences between the economic status of two-earner households and one-earner households. One of the critical differences between black two-earner households and white two-earner households is the greater proportion of total *family* income contributed by the female earner in black households. While this clearly has an effect on family functioning, such issues are not address because interactions among family members are not examined.

The report characterizes the four recessions between 1970 and 1982 as "government-induced," and though it recognizes these recessions as key factors, it fails, oddly, to consider the role of double-digit inflation. It fails to indicate that these government-induced slumps were employed as a means of reducing inflation, placing as a consequence the brunt of joblessness on low-income workers.

Social Trends

Most of the data analysis in chapter 10 repeats findings about demographic trends, fertility patterns, marital status, and living patterns that have been reported in many other studies. Thus it focuses on the disproportionate increases among blacks in the following areas: divorce rate, adolescent sexual activity, out-of-wedlock births, female-headed families, working mothers, and children in poverty. The analysis abstracts from the complexity of family structures in black communities. Only broad categories, i.e., two-parent families and single-parent families, are used.

Some assertions in chapter 10 are at variance with findings in chapter 6. For example, while chapter 10 devotes considerable space to challenging the "culture of poverty" thesis and the popular belief that welfare benefits contributed significantly to the rise in female-headed families and out-of-wedlock births among blacks, it also places great emphasis on the increase in female-headed families as an explanatory factor in the rise in black poverty. This assertion is in direct contradiction to findings in chapter 6, which indicate that the single-family structure was *not* a predominant factor in the rise in poverty among black families. There is also no mention in chapter 10 of the report's earlier finding (in chapter 6) that welfare assistance did not increase among black families throughout the 1970s and 1980s.

Interestingly, although the works of several black scholars are referenced in chapter 10, the conclusions of their studies often contradict the conclusions reached in the NRC study. For example, the report asserts that "African culture heritage...[is] far removed from the recent changes [in black family structure]," but cites no cross-cultural studies to support this conclusion. Yet research by Sudarkasa and other scholars have found strong evidence of African cultural continuities in contemporary African-American families.

Because of its peripheral interests in black families, the NRC report contributes very few insights about their functioning. It is mainly interested in accounting for changes in black family structure rather than family functioning. And even in its discussion of structure it is superficial. For example, no data is presented about changes in extended family households among blacks during the 1970s and 1980s. The fact that 90% of babies born out-of-wedlock to black teenagers live in three-generational households is conveniently omitted, despite an extensive discussion of adolescent pregnancies and births. Extended households are only addressed in the conclusion and then only in a very perfunctory fashion.

The NRC study also misrepresents important data on black female-headed families after the Great Depression. It asserts that "from 1940 to the late 1950s, the proportion of black families headed by a woman remained roughly constant at 19 percent" (p. 519). Yet, decennial census data reveals that the proportion of black female-headed families *fell* from 22.6% to 17.6% between 1940 and 1950.

Finally, the analysis fails to address the characteristics of black family residences and the changes in their characteristics over time. The characteristics of public and other low-income housing and variations in the accessibility of such housing clearly affect family functioning. There have been cyclical patterns of low-income housing construction over the 50-year period.

In sum, the thrust of the analysis–i.e., emphasizing similarities in the structure and functioning of black and white families as well as similarities in trends over time–leads to generalizations that obscure critical dimensions of African-American.

The failure to accord black families centrality in the NRC study is a continuing signal of the need for a solid base of Afro-centric research on the black family, research produced by scholars with knowledge of, and connection with, the traditions, values, and ethnics that permeate black lives.

Robert B. Hill is director of the Institute for Urban Research at Morgan State University, Baltimore; James B. Stewart is director of the Black Studies Program at Pennsylvania State University.

The Status of African-Americans: Convergence or Divergence?

James B. Stewart

Editor's Note: In this paper, Dr. Stewart is directing his remarks towards four papers presented at a session entitled "The National Research Council's Report on the Status of Black Americans 1940-1985," at the Allied Social Science Association meeting held in December of 1989 in Atlanta, Georgia. The authors of those papers were: Thomas Boston of Georgia Technological University; William Darity, Jr., of the University of North Carolina; Reynolds Farley of the University of Michigan; and James Heckman of Yale University. These papers were published in the May 1990 issue of the American Economic Review. *The full titles of the papers are included in the Reference section of this article.*

The frame of reference used in assessing the papers by Professors Farley, Heckman, Boston, and Darity[1] is shaped by my involvement as a member of the Trotter Institute Assessment Team.[2] This group conducted an investigation parallel to that made by the National Research Council (NRC).

The factors contributing to the existence of these two separate and distinct study groups are directly related to the issues raised in the paper by Boston. In considering the issue of the composition of the NRC study group his perspective derives more from what he calls the sociology of knowledge than from the politics of representation. In particular Boston refers to a critique implicit in Troy Duster's article, "Purpose and Bias,"[3] that emphasizes the criticality of examining the composition of a collaborative research team. Duster suggests that dissimilarities in ethnicity and social status between the group being studied and the research team are problematic. Although Boston stops short of the strict construction that only blacks can study blacks, he supports Du Bois's position that "research on black life in America must be brought back under the control fundamentally of African American institutions."[4] In keeping with this position the Trotter Institute organized a group of scholars, mostly but not exclusively African-American, to develop an alternative report to that of the NRC. The volumes generated through this effort can be obtained directly from the William Monroe Trotter Institute at the University of Massachusetts at Boston.

The papers presented in this session are connected to these two study groups in very different ways. Farley and Heckman contributed background papers for the NRC study, while Darity chaired one of the Trotter Institute task forces. Despite the divergence in perspectives it is possible to identify at least three questions that connect the four very different papers:

- What is the trajectory of the economic status of African-Americans?

- What factors are determining that trajectory?
- What are the limits of available analytical frameworks, data, and empirical techniques for identifying and quantifying trends and causal relationships?

These are critical questions. There is a need to assess past and present policies in the context of current trajectories so that new policies may be designed and implemented that can foster improvements in the status of African-Americans. In recent years these issues have taken on new significance as demographics have changed and as concerns about the relative competitiveness of the American labor force have heightened.

In addressing these questions, most scholars have tended to disaggregate the larger issues into smaller ones, so as to allow the application of sophisticated empirical techniques. However, the result has been that the answers generated are often even more narrowly focused than the questions. It is critical that empirical rigor not obscure the broader picture. In contrast, as concern turns to broader societal trends, efforts to quantify complex interactions are generally less successful than more restricted analyses. This occurs not only because the quality of "empirical" evidence deteriorates but also because conceptualizing the interactions among institutions and individual agents is difficult.

These two divergent approaches create a formidable incommensurability problem that can produce wholesale disjunctions in the assessment of social tendencies. It is this incommensurability that is reflected in the contrasts between the assessments in Darity's presentation and in the NRC report.

The title of the NRC report, *A Common Destiny*,[5] suggests an embedded ontology wherein the experiences and destinies of African-Americans and white Americans are inextricably interwoven and are steadily moving toward convergence. Although it is acknowledged in *A Common Destiny* that some stubborn inequalities persist and that the rate of convergence has slowed in recent years, it is suggested that a set of relatively minor policy changes is all that is needed to renew the convergence momentum.

The paper by Farley documents the persistence of racial inequality using 1980 data. This is the slowdown in convergence that *A Common Destiny* acknowledges. Farley's contribution is the desegregation of the so-called "white" population into ethnic subgroups. He finds that African-Americans lag behind all white ethnic groups with the exception of those that explicitly identify Native American ancestry. Farley's exclusion of immigrants from his analysis is, however, disappointing, since one of the most interesting issues raised by labor literature in recent years in how immigrants adjust to the American economy and how immigrants affect the earnings opportunities of African-Americans.

Further, while Farley notes the wide discrepancies between African-American men and other groups he shies away from a discussion of the implications of his findings. The potential significance can be seen from the work of various economists who have examined implications of immigration.6 Lucian Gatewood7 examines how European immigration historically displaced black artisans. The evidence on the impact of more recent immigration is mixed. One of the studies finding a negative effect on blacks is Stewart and Hyclak.8

It should also be noted that the papers by both Farley and Heckman examine only the experiences of males. Of course, caution should be exercised in assessments of African-American trends based only on sex-specific studies. In the case of immigrants, for example, MacPherson and Stewart9 demonstrate that economic adjustment of women differs significantly from that of men. Similar patterns hold true for domestic women. One of the best collections of material examining the economic status of African-American women is Simms and Malveaux.10

The NRC report's emphasis is on the measurement of outcomes rather than on an analysis of the forces producing these outcomes. The metrics highlighted in the NRC report–including educational attainments, geographical population distributions, and family size–support the convergence thesis. The principal data are taken from each of the decennial censuses since 1940. It is useful to consider some of the implications of the choice of data base for the convergence thesis. The thesis implies that the groups in question are interacting in what might be described as a "convergence regime." The concept of a convergence regime can be contrasted to what might be termed a "divergence regime." The term "convergence regime" is meant to describe the existence of a superstructure (i.e., a set of institutions) supportive of intergroup convergence. All institutions in this superstructure need not be committed to movement toward convergence, but those that affect status directly must not present insurmountable hurdles.

There is ongoing disagreement about what constitutes the set of institutions that have affected status most directly and/or have had the greatest influence on convergence/divergence. The institutions of special interest to economists are labor markets, educational institutions, and governments. It is critical to note that none of these institutions can affect an individual or a group's status independently. The situation of individuals or groups is shaped by the structural linkages among these institutions and the conditions of access to such institutions.

The problem is further complicated by the possibility of "regime shifts," shifts in the objective of the social order between achieving intergroup convergence and maintaining or expanding existing patterns of divergence. Misidentification of regime shifts can occur if it is assumed that such changes are perfectly correlated with changes in political status or in economic organization. It is possible for changes in either political status and/or economic structure to occur that improve the situation of a group without a change in the underlying social objective. An example of this phenomenon was the end of chattel slavery. Clearly Emancipation generated a change in the political status of African-Americans. In addition, with it the economic organization conditioning status was no longer plantation agriculture but share tenancy. However, the underlying social objective was not altered, as was demonstrated by the rapid demise of Reconstruction and the progressive reversal of laws protecting the new political status culminating in the *Plessy v. Ferguson* decision.

If a study of changes in the status of African-Americans had been undertaken in the 1880s covering the period 1840 to 1885, in all likelihood it would have interpreted observed changes as a regime shift and interpreted developments in the 1870s and early 1880s simply as outlying data points on a convergence trajectory. Subsequent developments, however, would have invalidated that interpretation.

This, then, is the problem facing convergence theorists. It must be possible to identify the timing of a shift from a historical pattern of divergence that clearly distinguishes these developments from the similar developments in the previous century cited above. If this cannot be done then it is more appropriate to characterize developments over the last 25 years as only a temporary departure from a long-run divergence trajectory.

Convergence theorists and empiricists have failed to demonstrate this regime shift. Rather, they have assumed that such a regime has been in existence, if not since the end of World War II, at least since the early 1950s with the beginning of the modern Civil Rights Movement, characterized by some as the "Second Reconstruction."

It is within the ontology of a convergence regime that Heckman explores the relative efficacy of education-labor market linkages and government-labor market linkages. He argues, correctly I believe, that civil rights legislation and enforcement contributed significantly to gains in the economic status of blacks during the period 1965 to 1975. The argument is not new; it was first advanced by King and Marshall in 1974.[11] The principal difference is that King and Marshall's documentation consisted solely of descriptive data while Heckman estimates a formal model using microdata. The particular significance of Heckman's analysis is that the findings contradict those of other studies that examine microdata and report that government action was of little consequence in contributing to changes. Other studies have argued that improvements in educational attainments and quality were the *deus ex machina* behind black progress during this period.

One of the reasons for the continuing disparagement of government action as a source of gains during this period is the absence of adequate measures of enforcement and enforcement effectiveness. Like most analysts, Heckman and his critics focus on federal enforcement efforts, which were admittedly weak. The use of metrics such as agency budgets and number of complaints filed convey almost no meaningful information. Their measures ignore state and local enforcement efforts, which are critical factors.

The need to focus on state and local enforcement in addition to federal enforcement is obvious. It was at these levels of government that African-Americans were most able to affect policy through electoral gains and through political action such as economic boycotts. Some useful work on enforcement of civil rights laws has been done by Landes[12] and Niemi.[13] One measure that could be added to typical specifications are dummy variables indicating whether a state had passed antidiscrimination legislation in a given year. However, even such a modification would not address a larger problem, i.e., the need for alternative theoretical treatments of government and extra-electoral political action as influences on public policy.

While mainstream economists have a strong preference for analytical investigations that focus on behaviors of individual agents, it is not clear that available empirical techniques can adequately capture the impact of structural parameters on individuals. This issue ties the preceding discussion directly to the concerns raised in the paper by Darity.

Darity implicitly suggests that the reality under investigation is a divergence regime rather than a convergence regime. He suggests even more poignantly that subsets of African-Americans may not survive culturally, or even physically, as global economics develop. The work of Wilhelm[14] is invoked to establish a precedent for this perspective. It is clear that both different descriptors and different types of data are required to examine such a "divergence regime." To illustrate, it is no accident that the NRC report explicitly avoids terminology such as "the underclass," "genocide," "endangered species," and so on, since this language is inconsistent with a "convergence regime" ontology. In a similar vein, studies conducted within the convergence regime ontology typically treat processes like migration and urbanization as innocuous developments, ignoring the disruptive results. The migration from the South in the 1950s was not a matter of choice; technological change in the form of the mechanical cotton picker and chemical fertilizers pushed blacks from the land by eliminating the need for cheap labor.

In a divergence regime the gains highlighted in the NRC report are compromises agreed to by controlling interests in the face of threats of direct action. Structural modifications and/or redistributions are designed to maintain existing patterns of dominance while reducing the threat of revolt. The reduction in threats to the ruling regime leads to retrenchment and retrogression.

In such a regime the class structure of the oppressed group is of critical importance because it determines the extent to which that group can protect itself against the action of the ruling regime and against structural changes in the global economic system. Darity goes further than most analysts in asserting that the continuing linkage between the fate of the African-American middle and working classes is a result of what he suggests is the disproportionate involvement of African-American managers in the oversight of support programs for the economically disadvantaged. His thesis is, however, consistent with the view advanced by Piven and Cloward[15] regarding the use of social support systems as mechanisms of social control.

Many of the issues addressed by Darity cannot be analyzed employing the same techniques used in studies that implicitly assume that the operative regime is convergence-oriented. With Darity's approach, however, there are some useful insights regarding long-term trends that can be gained. In addition, broader social questions can be generated by grounding the empirical analysis of trends related to race and ethnicity in long-cycle models (e.g., Kondratieff cycles) that endogenize major political developments and technological changes. (The classic study supporting recent work is Kondratieff.[16] Some of the representative studies of this genre include Bergsen, Goldstein, Rostow, Thompson, and van Duijn.[17]) Stewart[18] has attempted to extend such models to treat patterns of racial conflict as a function of the forces producing long cycles. That work takes the view of Arrow,[19] which is that it is possible to model black workers as producing something called "blackness" as well as goods as a point of departure. A household production framework is used to model interracial conflicts.

The principal implication of using long-cycle models is that such models can better capture extremely long-term trends of the type implied in the earlier allusion to similarities between the events of the last century and this century. To the extent that such long-term perspectives are better at describing processes of social change, studies exploring shorter time frames, including the NRC report, are potentially flawed if they do not locate the time frame under study at the appropriate point in an upswing or downturn in a longer cycle. This is in fact the approach to the study of African-Americans advocated by Du Bois as noted in the paper by Boston. Du Bois was a long-cycle theorist who suggested a century-long research project examining ten topics once every decade as the appropriate methodology to capture changes in the status of African-Americans.[20]

Whether one views social reality from the perspective of a convergence regime or a divergence regime there is agreement that trends in the 1980s have not been promising. Hopefully the publication of the NRC report and the Trotter Institute's series of volumes along with the papers discussed in this commentary will contribute to an increased focus on questions related to race and ethnicity. Hopefully such attention will include detailed examination of the work published in specialized organs that examine such issues on an ongoing basis, such as *The Review of Black Political Economy*. As such examinations proceed concurrent with the process of social change, it will be necessary to carry over W.E.B. Du Bois's characterization of "the problem of the color line" from the twentieth century into the twenty-first.

References

1. The titles of the papers presented at the session were as follows: Reynolds Farley, "Blacks, Hispanics and White Ethnic Groups: Are Blacks Uniquely Disadvantaged?"; James Heckman, "The Central Role of the South in Accounting for the Economic Progress of Black Americans"; Thomas Boston, "*A Common Destiny*: How Does It Compare to the Classic Studies of Black Life in America"; and William Darity, Jr., "Why Us?"

2. The formal title of this project was "The Assessment of the Status of Black Americans." Five study groups were organized to examine developments for African-Americans related to the following subjects: education; employment, income and occupations; health status and medical care; family; social and cultural change; and political participation and the administration of justice. The author served as a member of the study group on the family.

3. Duster, T. (1987). Purpose and Bias. *Society, 24* (2), 3.

4. Du Bois, W.E.B. (1968). *The Autobiography of W.E.B. Du Bois.* New York: International Publishers. P. 313.

5. Jaynes, G.D. & Williams, R.M., Jr. (Eds.). (1989). *A Common Destiny: Blacks and American Society.* Washington, DC: National Academy Press.

6. See for example: Borjas, G.J. (1985). Assimilation, Changes in Cohort Quality, and the Earnings of Immigrants. *Journal of Labor Economics, 3,* 463-489. Chiswick, B.R. (1978). The Effect of Americanization on the Earnings of Foreign-Born Men. *Journal of Political Economic, 86,* 897-922. Gatewood, L.B. (1974). The Black Artisan in the U.S., 1890-1930. *The Review of Black Political Economy, 5,* 19-44. Greenwood, M.J. & McDowell, J.M. (1986). The Factor Market Consequences of U.S. Immigration. *Journal of Economic Literature, 24,* 1738-1772. MacPherson, D.A. & Stewart, J.B. (1989). The Labor Force Participation and Earnings Profiles of Married Female Immigrants. *Quarterly Review of Economics and Business, 29,* 57-72. Stewart, J.B. & Hyclak, T. (1986). The Effect of Immigrants, Women, and Teenagers on the Relative Earnings of Black Males. *The Review of Black Political Economy, 15,* 93-101. Stewart, J.B. & Hyclak, T. (1984). An Analysis of the Earnings Profiles of Immigrants. *Review of Economics and Statistics, 66,* 292-296.

7. Gatewood, L.B. (1974). The Black Artisan in the U.S., 1890-1930. *The Review of Black Political Economy, 5,* 19-44.

8.   Stewart, J.B. & Hyclak, T. (1986). The Effect of Immigrants, Women, and Teenagers on the Relative Earnings of Black Males. *The Review of Black Political Economy, 15,* 93-101.

9.   MacPherson, D.A. & Stewart, J.B. (1989). The Labor Force Participation and Earnings Profiles of Married Female Immigrants. *Quarterly Review of Economics and Business, 29,* 57-72.

10. Simms, M.C. & Malveaux, J. (Eds.). (1986). *Slipping Through the Cracks: The Status of Black Women.* New Brunswick, NJ: Transaction Books.

11. King, A.G. & Marshall, R. (1974). Black-White Economic Convergence and the Civil Rights Act of 1964. *Labor Law Journal, 25,* 462-471.

12. Landes, W.M. (1968). The Economics of Fair Employment Laws. *Journal of Political Economy, 76,* 507-552.

13. Niemi, A.W., Jr. (1974). Impact of Recent Civil Rights Laws. *The American Journal of Economics and Sociology, 33,* 137-144.

14. Wilhelm, S. (1970). *Who Needs the Negro?* Cambridge, MA: Shenkman Publishing.

15. Piven, F.F. & Cloward, R. (1971). *Regulating the Poor: The Function of Public Welfare.* New York: Pantheon Books.

16. Kondratieff, N. (1935). The Long Wave in Economic Life. *The Review of Economics and Statistics, 42,* 105-115.

17. Bergsen, A. (1985). Cycles of War in the Reproduction of the World Economy. In P.M. Johnson & W.R. Thompson (Eds.), *Rhythms in Politics and Economics* (pp. 313-331). New York: Praeger. Goldstein, J.S. (1988). *Long Cycles: Prosperity and War in the Modern Age.* New Haven: Yale University Press. Rostow, W.W. (1975). Kondratieff, Schumpeter, and Kuznets: Trend Periods Revisited. *Journal of Economic History, 35,* 719-753. Thompson, W.R. & Zuk, L.G. (1982). War, Inflation, and the Kondratieff Long Wave. *Journal of Conflict Resolution, 26,* 621-644. VanDuijn, J. (1983). *The Long Wave in Economic Life.* Boston: Allen and Unwin.

18. Stewart, J.B. (1988). Kondratieff Cycles and the Political-Economic Status of Blacks in the United States. Mimeographed.

19.   Arrow, K. (1974). The Theory of Discrimination. In O. Ashenfelter & A. Rees, (Eds.), *Discrimination in Labor Markets* (pp. 3-33). Princeton, NJ: Princeton University Press.

20.   Du Bois, W.E.B. (1900). To the Nations of the World. *Report of the Pan-African Conference.* London: Pan-African Conference.

James B. Stewart is director of the Black Studies Program at Pennsylvania State University.

Appendix

Assessment of the Status of African-Americans
Project Study Group Members

Project Leaders

Director: Wornie L. Reed, William Monroe Trotter Institute, University of
Massachusetts at Boston

Co-Chair: James E. Blackwell, Department of Sociology, University of
Massachusetts at Boston

Co-Chair: Lucius J. Barker, Department of Political Science, Washington University

Study Group on Education

Charles V. Willie (Chair), School of Education, Harvard University
Antoine M. Garibaldi (Vice-Chair), Department of Education, Xavier University
Robert A. Dentler, Department of Sociology, University of Massachusetts at Boston
Robert C. Johnson, Minority Studies Academic Program, St. Cloud State University
Meyer Weinberg, Department of Education, University of Massachusetts at Amherst

Study Group on Employment, Income and Occupations

William Darity, Jr., (Chair) Department of Economics, University of North Carolina
Barbara Jones (Vice-Chair), College of Business, Prairies View A&M University
Jeremiah P. Cotton, Department of Economics, University of Massachusetts at
Boston
Herbert Hill, Industrial Relations Research Institute, University of Wisconsin

Study Group on Political Participation and
the Administration of Justice

Michael B. Preston (Chair), Department of Political Science, University of Southern
California
Diane M. Pinderhughes (Vice-Chair), Department of Political Science, University of
Illinois/Champaign
Tobe Johnson, Department of Political Science, Morehouse College

Nolan Jones, Staff Director, Committee on Criminal Justice and Public Protection, National Governors Association

Susan Welch, Department of Political Science, University of Nebraska

John Zipp, Department of Sociology, University of Wisconsin-Milwaukee

Study Group on Social and Cultural Change

Alphonso Pinkney (Chair), Department of Sociology, Hunter College

James Turner (Vice-Chair), Africana Studies and Research Center, Cornell University

John Henrik Clarke, Department of Black and Puerto Rican Studies, Hunter College

Sidney Wilhelm, Department of Sociology, State University of New York-Buffalo

Study Group on Health Status and Medical Care

William Darity, Sr. (Chair), School of Public Health, University of Massachusetts at Amherst

Stanford Roman (Vice-Chair), Morehouse School of Medicine, Atlanta

Claudia Baquet, National Cancer Institute, Bethesda, Maryland

Noma L. Roberson, Department of Cancer Control and Epidemiology, Rockwell Park Institute

Study Group on the Family

Robert B. Hill (Chair), Morgan State University, Baltimore, Maryland

Andrew Billingsley (Vice-Chair), Department of Family and Community Development, University of Maryland

Eleanor Engram, Engram-Miller Associates, Cleveland, Ohio

Michelene R. Malson, School of Social Work, University of North Carolina

Roger H. Rubin, Department of Family and Community Development, University of Maryland

Carol B. Stack, Graduate School of Education, University of California-Berkeley

James B. Stewart, Black Studies Program, Pennsylvania State University

James E. Teele, Department of Sociology, Boston University